Everyday English

STUDENT BOOK

2A

Food   Clothes   Transportation   Post Office   School

Original by Johnnie Prather and the Asian Newcomer Parent Program

| Edited by | Linda Schurer |
| Illustrated by | Elliotte Mao |

Alemany Press

Prentice Hall Regents, Englewood Cliffs, NJ 07632

Printed in the United States of America

10 9 8 7 6 5 4 3 2 1

ISBN 0-13-292400-5

Prentice-Hall International (UK) Limited, *London*
Prentice-Hall of Australia Pty. Limited, *Sydney*
Prentice-Hall Canada Inc., *Toronto*
Prentice-Hall Hispanoamericana, S.A., *Mexico*
Prentice-Hall of India Private Limited, *New Delhi*
Prentice-Hall of Japan, Inc., *Tokyo*
Simon & Schuster Asia Pte. Ltd., *Signapore*
Editora Prentice-Hall do Brasil, Ltda., *Rio de Janeiro*

PREFACE

This second edition of EVERYDAY ENGLISH is derived from the original materials of that name which were developed by the Asian Newcomer Parent Program (ANPP) in San Francisco under a HEW/ABE grant funded through the Education Center for Chinese. The revised edition came about because of the continued requests by teachers, schools and programs for a reappearance of EVERYDAY ENGLISH. The original format has been maintained, but the content has been updated and generalized, and the Student Books have been expanded.

EVERYDAY ENGLISH is the result of the work of the creative and dedicated staff of the ANPP, which originally produced it in 1973. I would like to express my deepest gratitude and indebtedness to Johnnie Prather, curriculum writer, who originally wrote these materials. I would further like to thank the entire staff of the ANPP, including: Joyce Carrillo, Linda Malila-Krauskopf, Harrison Lim, Jacqueline Liu, Pauline Luk, Elliotte Mao, Victoria Low Oei, June M. Quan, Sheryl Reiser, K. Lynn Savage, William Sinclair, Robert L. Smithton, Kay Lum Szeto, Betty Lee Wong, Eleanor Wong and consultants Dorothy Danielson and Dr. Daniel Glicksberg.

I am also indebted to the Board of Governors of the Education Center for Chinese, chaired by Judge Harry W. Low, for its support of this edition, and to the San Francisco Community College District, particularly the Chinatown/North Beach and the Alemany Centers, for their continuous support of EVERYDAY ENGLISH.

It would be impossible to name all of the individual teachers, program coordinators and students who have contributed their suggestions to these revised materials. However, I would particularly like to thank Nina Gibson and Marge Ryder for their constant support, wealth of ideas, insightful criticisms and proofreading skills. I would also like to thank Ken Beck, Jacqueline Liu, Victoria Oei, Judy and Roger E. Winn-Bell Olsen, Lynn Savage and Nancy Thomas for their many helpful suggestions and ideas on this revision, and Elliotte Mao, for again providing her clever and imaginative illustrations. I am especially grateful to June Quan, former project director, whose support, encouragement, advice and inspiration made this edition of EVERYDAY ENGLISH possible.

Finally, I would like to thank all of the teachers and students whose enthusiastic responses to the original EVERYDAY ENGLISH inspired this edition.

Linda Schurer
July, 1980

FOOD

1   This is an American supermarket. Supermarkets sell everything.

2   They sell food to eat.

3   They sell liquor and wine to drink.

4   They sell cigarettes to smoke.

5   They sell books to read.

6   They sell soap to clean your house and your dishes.

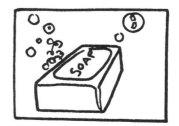

FOOD

READ

I shop at the supermarket.

I buy food, wine, and books.

I eat the food.

I drink the wine.

I read the books and magazines.

PRACTICE

I		
We	eat	food.
You		
They		

READ

This is my neighbor.

He goes to the supermarket, too.

He buys food, cigarettes and soap.

He eats the food.

He smokes the cigarettes.

He uses the soap.

PRACTICE

He		
She	eat<u>s</u>	the food.

FILL IN THE BLANKS

1. I __*eat*__ food.

2. My neighbor _____ food.

3. You _____ soap.

4. She _____ soap.

5. They _____ cigarettes.

6. He _____ wine.

7. We _____ books.

8. I _____

I don't buy wine.

He doesn't buy wine.

| I
We
You
They | don't | buy wine. | He
She | doesn't | buy wine. |

don't = do not

doesn't = does not

WRITE SENTENCES

don't	food	wine	books
doesn't	cigarettes	liquor	soap
	magazines	brandy	

1. I *don't buy cigarettes.*

2. He _____

3. We _____

4. They _____

5. She _____

6. You _____

7. _____

3

Two Neighbors

     1.   Do you buy wine?

     2.   Yes, I do

     1.   Where?

     2.   At the supermarket.

PRACTICE

   Do you buy wine?

liquor store

     <u>Yes</u>, I <u>do</u>.
     <u>No</u>, I <u>don't</u>.

   Where?   At the supermarket.
              At the discount store.
              At the liquor store.
              At the bookstore.

WRITE CONVERSATIONS

1.   Do you buy _____?

2.   Yes, I do.

1.   Where?

2.   At the _____.

discount store

1.   Do you _____?

2.   Yes, _____.

1.   Where?

2.   _____ _____

bookstore

FOOD

CONVERSATIONS   Two Neighbors

1.   Do you buy soap at the supermarket?

2.   No, I don't.

1.   Where do you buy it?

2.   At the discount store.

1.   Do you buy books at the supermarket?

2.   No, I don't.

1.   Where do you buy them?

2.   At the bookstore.

PRACTICE

| Where do you buy | food?
soap?
wine? | I buy <u>it</u> at the supermarket. |

| Where do you buy | magazines?
books?
cigarettes? | I buy <u>them</u> at the supermarket. |

WRITE CONVERSATIONS

1.   Do you buy _____ at the supermarket?

2.   No, I _____.

1.   Where do you buy _____?

2.   _____

1.   Do you buy _____ at the _____?

2.   No, _____.

1.   Where_____?

2.   _____

To A Neighbor

1. I need some wine.

2. Go to the supermarket.

1. Does the supermarket sell wine?

2. Yes, it does.
   It sells everything.

PRACTICE

Does | he / she | need wine?   Yes, | he / she | does.

Does it sell wine?   Yes, it does.

Do | they / you / we / I | need wine?   Yes, | they / I / we / you | do.

WRITE QUESTIONS AND ANSWERS

1. *Does* the supermarket sell cigarettes?   *Yes, it does.*

2. _____ you need magazines?   _____

3. _____ they need soap?   _____

4. _____ she buy wine?   _____

5. _____   _____

6. _____   _____

7. _____   _____

8. _____   _____

A good supermarket sells almost everything.

But it doesn't sell everything.

It doesn't sell cars.

It doesn't sell furniture.

It doesn't sell clothes.

PRACTICE

Does the supermarket sell cars?   No, it doesn't.

Does | he / she | buy liquor?   No, | he / she | doesn't.

ANSWER THE QUESTIONS

1. Does the supermarket sell cars?   *No, it doesn't.*

2. Does the supermarket sell furniture?   _____

3. Does the supermarket sell clothes?   _____

4. Does the supermarket sell food?   _____

5. Does the supermarket sell soap?   _____

6. Do you go to the supermarket?   _____

7. Do you buy wine?   _____

READ THE STORY

I'm going to the supermarket. I need some potatoes, some onions and some tomatoes. Potatoes, onions and tomatoes aren't expensive. I'm not taking much money.

PRACTICE

| I need | a potato.
a tomato.
an onion. | I need | some potatoes.
some tomatoes.
some onions. |

FILL IN THE BLANKS

a   an   some

1. I need ___*a*___ tomato.

2. I need _____ potatoes.

3. I need _____ onions.

4. I need _____ potato.

5. I need _____ carrot.

6. I need _____ peas.

7. I need _____ beans.

8. I need _____ apple.

WRITE ABOUT YOU

I'm going to the supermarket.

I need _____, _____, and

_____.

_____, _____, and

_____ aren't expensive. I'm not taking much money.

FOOD

I'm going to the supermarket. I need some meat. I want some beef and some pork. I want some fish and some chicken, too. Meat is expensive. I'm taking a lot of money.

PRACTICE

I need <u>some</u> | meat.
  | beef.
  | pork.
  | chicken.

FILL IN THE BLANKS

               a   an   some

1. I need *some* beef.
2. I need _____ chicken.
3. I need _____ potato.
4. I need _____ onions.
5. I need _____ meat.

6. I want _____ apple.
7. I want _____ coffee.
8. I want _____ tomatoes.
9. I want _____ pork.
10. I want _____ fish.

WRITE A STORY
What do you need?

I'm going to the supermarket today.

I need _____.

I want _____.

_____ expensive.

I'm taking _____ money.

9

WRITE THE NAMES

1 *peas*

2 *carrots*

3 _____

4 _____

5 _____

6 _____

7 _____

8 _____

9 _____

10 _____

11 _____

12 _____

13 _____

14 _____

15 _____

16 _____

17 _____

18

_____

19

_____

20

_____

21

_____

22

_____

23

_____

24

_____

25

_____

26

_____

27

_____

28

_____

29

_____

30

_____

31

_____

32

_____

CONVERSATION   Customer and Clerk In The Store

    1.   I need some salt.

    2.   Sorry, we're out of salt.

    1.   You don't have any salt?

    2.   No, we don't.
          But we'll have some tomorrow.

PRACTICE

They have <u>some</u>	salt. pepper. oil.	They <u>don't</u> have <u>any</u>	bread. rice. peas.

We'll I'll You'll They'll He'll She'll	have some tomorrow.

FILL IN THE BLANKS

                    some   any

1. We need _____*some*_____ salt.

2. I don't have _____ pepper.

3. She wants _____ bread.

4. She doesn't have _____ rice.

5. They need _____ oil.

6. I don't need _____ soup.

7. I need _____

8. I don't need _____

FOOD

<u>To The Clerk</u>

1.   Do you have any frozen peas?

2.   No, we don't.
     But we have some canned peas.

1.   I don't like canned peas.

2.   We have some fresh peas, too.

1.   No, thank you.
     Fresh peas are a lot of trouble.

PRACTICE

Do you have <u>any</u> frozen peas?   Yes, we do.
                                             No, we don't.

I don't like	canned peas.
	frozen peas.
	fresh peas.

Fresh	peas	are a lot of trouble.
	beans	
	potatoes	

fresh   frozen   canned

WRITE A CONVERSATION

1.   Do you have _____?

2.   No, we _____. But we have _____.

1.   I don't like _____.

2.   We have some _____, too.

1.   No, thank you. _____a lot of trouble.

Two Friends At Work

    1.   I'm hungry. I want a hamburger.

    2.   Go to the restaurant on the corner.

    1.   Do they have good hamburgers?

    2.   Yes, And you get a lot of potato chips, too.

PRACTICE

  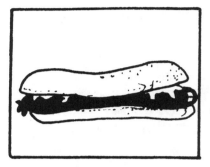

I want <u>a</u> hamburger.   I want <u>a</u> coke.   I want <u>a</u> hot dog.

I want <u>some</u> spaghetti. I want <u>some</u> potato chips. I want <u>some</u> french fries.

WRITE A CONVERSATION

    1.   I'm hungry. I want _____.

    2.   Go to _____

    1.   Do they have good _____?

    2.   Yes, and you get _____, too.

            FOOD

Two Friends On The Street

1.   I have to go to the store.
     Please come with me.

2.   Will it take long?

1.   No. Just a few minutes.

2.   O. K. I'll go.

PRACTICE

| I
We
You
They | have to   go. | He
She | has to   go. |

I have to go.
   Come with me.

We have to go.
   Come with us.

She has to go.
   Go with her.

He has to go.
   Go with him.

They have to go.
   Go with them.

WRITE SENTENCES

| have to | me | her | us |
| has to | him | them | |

1. I _have to_ go to the store. Please come with _me_   .

2. He_____go to the store. Please go with_____.

3. They _____go to the store. Please go with _____.

4. She _____go to the store. Please go with _____.

5. We _____go to the store. Please come with _____.

6. _____go to the store. Please _____.

<u>W</u>ill it take long?

<u>Yes</u>, it <u>will</u>.

<u>No</u>, it <u>won't</u>.

Will you go with | me?
him?
her?
them?
us?

<u>Yes</u>, I <u>will</u>.

<u>No</u>, I <u>won't</u>.

WRITE CONVERSATIONS

1. I _____ go to the store.

    Please come with _____.

2. _____ it take long?

1. No, it _____.

    Just _____

1. He_____ go to the store.

    Please go with_____.

2. _____ it take _____?

1. Yes, it _____.

2. Sorry, I_____ have time.

1. They _____ go to the store.
    Please go with _____.

2. _____?

1. _____

2. _____

Two Friends Look At The Ads

1. How much is chicken at _____?

2. It's _____ a pound.

1. How much is it at _____?

2. It's _____ a pound.

1. How much are oranges at _____?

2. They're _____ pounds for _____

1. How much are apples?

2. They're _____ pounds for _____

PRACTICE

How much is chicken?
        beef?
        pork?

It's $_____ a pound.

How much are apples?
        bananas?
        oranges?

They're _____ pounds for $_____

LOOK AT THE ADS IN THE NEWSPAPER
WRITE THE NAMES OF 2 STORES

_____   _____

1. How much is chicken?   It's $_____ a pound at _____
                        It's $_____ a pound at _____

2. How much are apples?   They're ____ pounds for $_____ at_____
                        They're ____ pounds for $_____ at_____

3. How much is beef?   _____

                        _____

4. How much are oranges?   _____

                        _____

Husband and Wife

1. You should shop at _____tomorrow.

2. Why?

1. They have good specials this week.
   Chicken is only $_____a pound.

2. O. K. I'll go early tomorrow morning.

PRACTICE

| I
We
They
You
He
She | should | shop at _____tomorrow. |

WRITE
Where do you shop?
Write the names of the stores.

_____   _____

_____   _____

LOOK AT THE NEWSPAPER ADS
Where should you shop this week?

1. I *should* shop at _____this week.

    _____is only $_____a pound.

2. We _____shop at _____this week.

    _____only _____pounds for $_____

3. You _____shop at _____this week.

    _____

4. I_____

    _____   _____

At the check-out stand, listen to the clerk and watch the cash register. Sometimes the clerk makes a mistake.

2 for 39.
2 pounds at 20¢ a pound.
59.
3 for a dollar.
That's $2.38 total.

.39
.40
.59
$1.00
$2.38

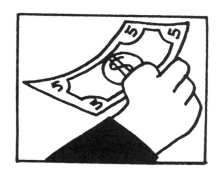

Here's $5.00.

$2.38 -- .39
.40
.50
.75
$3.00
4.00
5.00 Thank you. Come again.

CONVERSATION   At The Check-out Stand

1. You gave me the wrong change.

2. Are you sure?

1. Yes, You owe me a dollar.

2. You're right. I'm sorry.

1. That's O. K.

CONVERSATIONS

At The Check-out Stand

1. I forgot to buy apples.
   Go get me some.

2. How many do you want?

1. Five or six.

2. O. K.

At The Meat Counter

1. I want some ground beef.

2. O. K. How much do you want?

1. A pound and a half.

2. Here you are.
   Pay the cashier.

PRACTICE

How many	apples bananas onions	do you want?	Five. Ten. A dozen.

How much	meat pork shrimp beef	do you want?	A pound. A pound and a half. Two pounds. Two and a half pounds.

WRITE CONVERSATIONS

1. Get me some _____

2. How _____ do you want?

1. _____

2. _____

1. I need some _____

2. How _____ do you want?

1. _____

2. _____

Mother To Child

1. Will you go to the store for me?

2. O. K. What do you want?

1. A bottle of peanut oil, a box of soap and a can of peaches.

2. Oil, soap and peaches. Anything else?

1. No, that's all.

PRACTICE

a bottle of | soy sauce
 | peanut oil
  | beer
  | catsup

a box of | soap
 | cereal
  | crackers

a can of | milk
 | peaches
  | corn

a jar of | peanut butter
 | pickles
  | jam

FILL IN THE BLANKS   bottle   box   can   jar

1. I want a *bottle* of peanut oil.

2. I want a _____ of soap.

3. She wants a _____ of milk.

4. He needs a _____ of cereal.

5. You need a _____ of pickles.

6. She needs a _____ of peas.

7. I need a _____ of _____.

8. I need a _____.

9. I _____.

FOOD

Betty went to the supermarket yesterday. She doesn't have time to shop every day so she bought a lot of things. Now she doesn't have to shop every day.

PRACTICE

She <u>goes</u> to the supermarket <u>every day</u>.

She <u>went</u> to the supermarket <u>yesterday</u>.

She <u>buys</u> a lot of things <u>every day</u>.

She <u>bought</u> a lot of things <u>last week</u>.

WRITE
Betty bought these things at the supermarket.
Write sentences about Betty.

1. *She bought vegetables yesterday.*
2. _____
3. _____
4. _____
5. _____
6. _____

I went to the supermarket this morning. I needed some shrimp. The supermarket was out of shrimp. I wanted some fresh broccoli, too. They didn't have any fresh broccoli. I didn't buy anything.

PRACTICE

I		
He		
She		
We	needed	some shrimp yesterday.
You	wanted	
They		

It was out of | shrimp | yesterday.
broccoli
peas

FINISH THE SENTENCES

1. I _wanted_ some shrimp yesterday.

    The supermarket _was_ out of shrimp.

2. He _____ some rice last week.

    The supermarket _____ out of rice.

3. She _____ some _____ yesterday.

    The supermarket _____

4. They _____ some _____

    The supermarket _____

5. _____

    _____

They	didn't have any	broccoli shrimp oil	yesterday.

<u>Did</u> she <u>go</u> to the supermarket yesterday?

<u>Yes</u>, she <u>did</u>.
<u>No</u>, she <u>didn't</u>.

<u>Did</u>	she he I we you they	<u>go</u>	yesterday?

ANSWER THE QUESTIONS

1. Did you go to the supermarket yesterday?   *Yes, I did.*

2. Did you buy a lot of things?   _____

3. Did you buy rice?   _____

4. Did you buy coffee?   _____

5. Did you buy cigarettes?   _____

WRITE A STORY ABOUT YOU

I *went* to the supermarket _____.

I _____ some _____, _____, and _____

The supermarket was out of _____.

They didn't have any _____. I didn't buy any_____.

American supermarkets _are_ convenient. They _____ a
(1)   (2)
lot of things. They _____ food, liquor, magazines and cigarettes.
(3)
Sometimes _____ sell books, too.
(4)

Supermarkets are usually _____. Sometimes they
(5)
_____ very busy. But Americans _____ them. _____ can
(6)   (7)   (8)
buy everything in one place.

Mrs. Choy _____ like supermarkets. They _____ too far from
(9)   (10)
her house. She _____ to go to the small stores in her neighborhood.
(11)
She _____ buy a lot of things in one place. She _____ a
(12)   (13)
little in this store and a little in that store.

ANSWER THE QUESTIONS

1. Are American supermarkets convenient?   _Yes, they are._

2. Do they sell a lot of things?   _____

3. Do they sell food and liquor?   _____

4. Are supermarkets usually small?   _____

5. Are supermarkets busy?   _____

6. Do Americans like supermarkets?   _____

7. Why?   _____

8. Does Mrs. Choy like supermarkets?   _____

9. Why?   _____

10. Does she like small stores?   _____

CLOTHES

CONVERSATION   <u>Mrs. Tran and A Friend</u>

1. I need some material.

2. The fabric store sells material.

1. I need some needles and thread, too.

2. The fabric store sells everything
    for sewing.

PRACTICE

She needs | a pattern.
          | a zipper.
          | thread.
          | material.

She needs | some material.
          | some thread.
          | some needles.
          | some buttons.

FILL IN THE BLANKS

                    a   some

1. She needs *some* buttons.

2. She needs _____ pattern.

3. She needs _____ thread.

4. She needs _____ material.

5. She needs _____ zipper.

WRITE A CONVERSATION

1. I need _____.

2. The fabric store _____.

1. I need _____, too.

2. The fabric store _____.

CLOTHES

CONVERSATION

<u>Mrs. Tran and A Friend</u>

1. Does the fabric store sell scissors?

2. Yes, it does.
   It sells everything for sewing.

1. Does it sell clothes?

2. No, it doesn't.
   The department store sells clothes.

PRACTICE

<u>Does</u> | he
it
she | sell clothes?

<u>Yes</u>, | he
it
she | <u>does</u>.   <u>No</u>, | he
it
she | <u>doesn't</u>.

*WRITE QUESTIONS AND ANSWERS
ABOUT THE FABRIC STORE*

1. *Does the fabric store sell clothes?*
   No, it doesn't.

2. _____

   _____

3. _____

   _____

CONVERSATIONS   To The Clerk

   1.   Do you have this pattern?

   2.   Yes, we do. What size?

   1.   Size 10.

   2.   Here it is.

   1.   Do you have this pattern?

   2.   Yes, we do, but we don't have
        every size.

   1.   Do you have size 10?

   2.   No, we don't.
        I'm sorry.

PRACTICE

| Do | you
we
they | have this pattern? | Yes,

No, | I
you
they | do.

don't. |

WRITE QUESTIONS AND ANSWERS

1. (you, pattern)   *Do you have this pattern* ?
    Yes, *we do* .

2. (they, thread) _____
    No, _____.

3. (you, buttons) _____
    Yes, _____.

4. (they, size 8) _____
    No, _____.

5. (you, size 14) _____
    Yes, _____.

CLOTHES

To The Clerk

1. This material is beautiful.
   What is it?

2. It's silk.

1. Is it washable?

2. No, it isn't.
   Dry clean only.

PRACTICE

These are fabrics

| silk | acrylic | wool | dacron |
| cotton | nylon | polyester | rayon |

These are washing instructions

handwash

machine wash

dry clean

WRITE CONVERSATIONS

1. This material is beautiful. What is it?

2. It's _____

1. Is it washable?

2. _____

1. This material is beautiful.
   What is it?

2. _____

1. _____?

2. _____

CLOTHES

This is a label on a shirt.

60% cotton	40% dacron
Wash and wear	No ironing

ANSWER THE QUESTIONS

1. Is it washable?   *Yes, it is.*
2. Does it need ironing?   *No, it doesn't.*
3. Is it easy to wash? _____
4. What is the material? _____

READ THE LABEL

65% cotton	35% polyester
Hand wash	Cool iron

1. What is the material? _____
2. Is it easy to wash? _____
3. Does it need ironing? _____

READ THE LABEL

100% Wool
Dry clean only

1. What is the material? _____
2. Is it washable? _____

LOOK AT THE LABEL ON YOUR DRESS OR SHIRT

1. Is it washable? _____
2. What is the material? _____
3. Does it need ironing? _____

To The Clerk

1. This striped material is very pretty.
    Is it washable?

2. Yes, it is.
    It's polyester and it's easy to wash.

1. Does it need ironing?

2. No, it doesn't.

1. How much is it?

2. $ 3.00 a yard.

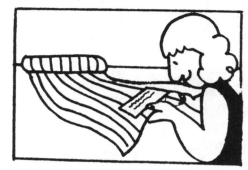

PRACTICE

striped   plaid   print   solid color   polka dot

WRITE QUESTIONS TO ASK THE CLERK IN THE FABRIC STORE

1. *Is this material washable* _____ ?

2. _____ ?

3. _____ ?

4. _____ ?

5. _____ ?

6. _____ ?

7. _____ ?

8. _____ ?

<u>To The Clerk</u>

        1.   I want this material.

        2.   How much do you want?

        1.   A yard and a half.

        2.   O. K.

FILL IN THE BLANKS

1.   A yard is   __36__ inches.

2.   ½ yard is   _____ inches.

3.   ¼ yard is   _____ inches.

4. 1/3 yard is   _____ inches.

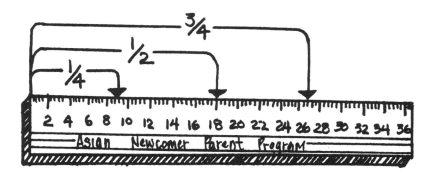

COMPARE

        How much is it?
           It's $ 2.00 a yard.

        How much do you want?
           Two yards.

WRITE CONVERSATIONS

1.   I want this material.

2. _____?

1.   2 ½ yards.

2. _____

                    1.   I want this material.

                       _____?

                    2. $ 5.00 a yard.

                    1.   _____

                                    CLOTHES

Men ___*do*___ not _____ sew and they do
     (1)   (2)

_____ buy material. But they _____ their
  (3)   (4)

own _____ and they _____ to know
      (5)   (6)

sizes and material.

PRACTICE

always	=	100%
usually	=	90%
often	=	50% - 90%
sometimes	=	20% - 60%
never	=	0%

FINISH THE SENTENCES

      always   usually   often   sometimes   never

1. I _____ buy my own clothes.

2. I _____ buy material.

3. I _____ sew.

4. My husband _____ buys his own clothes.

5. My wife _____ sews her own clothes.

6. My children _____ buy their own clothes.

7. _____ expensive material.

8. _____ wash and wear clothes.

9. _____

10. _____

<u>To The Clerk</u>

1. I need a pair of pants.

2. These are nice. They are wool,
    and they don't wrinkle.

1. Are they washable?

2. No, they aren't. Dry clean only.

1. I need a dress.

2. This is nice. It is polyester,
    and it doesn't wrinkle.

1. Is it washable?

2. Yes, it is. Machine wash.

PRACTICE

a dress

a blouse

a shirt

a pair of shoes

a pair of tennis shoes

a pair of socks

a pair of boots

a suit

a sweater

a coat

a raincoat

a pantsuit

a pair of pants

a pair of jeans

CONVERSATION   Mr. Perez Talks To The Clerk

    1.   I need a pair of pants.

    2.   What size do you wear?

    1.   33 waist, 30 length.

    2.   These are nice and they are wash and wear.

    1.   I'll try them on.

MEASURE

MEN

neck _____

arms _____

waist_____

length_____

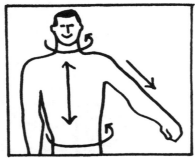

WOMEN

bust _____

waist _____

hips _____

SIZE CHART FOR WOMEN'S DRESSES

BUST	31½"	32½"	34"	36"	38"
WAIST	24"	25"	26½"	28"	30"
HIPS	33½"	34½"	36"	38"	40"
SIZE	8	10	12	14	16

What size do you wear?   _____

<u>To The Clerk In The Department Store</u>

1. Is this dress on sale?

2. Yes, it is. It's 25% off.

1. How much is it?

2. It's $30 now. It was $40.

COMPARE

ON SALE   --   It was $40.

Now it's $30.

FOR SALE   --   Somebody wants to sell it.

WRITE CONVERSATIONS

1. Is this shirt on sale?

2. Yes, _____. It's _____% off.

1. How much is it?

2. It's $_____ now. It was $_____.

1. Is this _____?

2. Yes,_____. It's _____off.

1. How _____?

2. It's _____ now.

It was _____.

CLOTHES

Mrs. Lane Returns a Shirt

    1.   I want to return this shirt.

    2.   What's wrong?

    1.   My husband doesn't like it.

    2.   O.K. I'll give you a refund.

PRACTICE

My <u>husband</u> doesn't like <u>this shirt</u>.
    <u>He</u> doesn't like <u>it</u>.

My <u>daughter</u> doesn't like <u>these gloves</u>.
    <u>She</u> doesn't like <u>them</u>.

My <u>children</u> don't like <u>these shoes</u>.
    <u>They</u> don't like <u>them</u>.

WRITE SENTENCES

       he   it
       she   them
       they

1. My husband doesn't like this shirt.

    He doesn't like it.

2. My wife doesn't like this coat.

    _____

3. My son doesn't like these jeans.

    _____

4. My daughter doesn't like this sweater.

    _____

5. My children don't like these shoes.

    _____

6. My friend doesn't like this jacket.

    _____

CLOTHES

CONVERSATIONS   In The Department Store

1.   I want to return these jeans.

2.   Do you have the sales slip?

1.   Yes, here it is.

2.   O.K.   I can give you a refund.

1.   I want to return these pants.

2.   Do you have the sales slip?

1.   No, I don't.

2.   I'm sorry.   I can't give you a refund.
     You have to have the sales slip.

PRACTICE

Do you <u>have</u> the sales slip?

     Yes, here it is.
     No, I don't.

I <u>can</u> give you a refund.
I <u>can't</u> give you a refund.

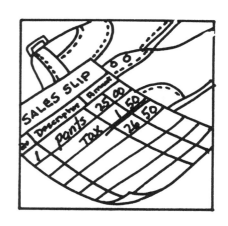

You <u>have to have</u> the sales slip.
He <u>has to have</u> the sales slip.

WRITE A CONVERSATION

1.   I want to return _____

2.   Do you _____the sales slip?

1.   _____

2.   _____

     _____

Two Friends

1.   I went shopping yesterday.

2.   Did you go downtown?

1.   Yes, I did.

2.   Did you buy anything?

1.   Yes, I did.   I bought a shirt for my husband.

COMPARE

   I <u>go</u> shopping <u>every day</u>.   I <u>buy</u> something <u>every day</u>.
        I <u>went</u> shopping <u>yesterday</u>.   I <u>bought</u> something yesterday.

PRACTICE

Did	you we they he she	go downtown <u>yesterday</u>?	Yes,	I you they he she	<u>did</u>.

I bought a shirt for <u>my husband</u>.   I bought a shirt for <u>him</u>.
I bought a dress for <u>my daughter</u>.   I bought a dress for <u>her</u>.
I bought shoes for <u>my son and daughter</u>.   I bought shoes for <u>them</u>.

WRITE SENTENCES

1.   I went shopping for my daughter.

   I bought a dress for her.

2.   I went shopping for my son.

   _____

3.   I went shopping for _____

   _____

4.   I went shopping for _____

   _____

CLOTHES

Two Friends

  1. Were you at home yesterday afternoon?

  2. No, I wasn't.
      I went shopping.

  1. Did you buy anything?

  2. No, I didn't.
      Everything was too expensive.

PRACTICE

Were | you / we / they | at home yesterday?   Was | he / she | at home yesterday?

Yes, | I / he / she | was.   Yes, | you / we / they | were.

READ THE CONVERSATION
ANSWER THE QUESTIONS

  1. Was she home yesterday?   *No, she wasn't.*

  2. Did she go shopping yesterday?   _____

  3. Did she go shopping yesterday morning? _____

  4. Did she buy anything?   _____

  5. Why not?   _____

  6. Was she at the store yesterday?   _____

  7. Were you at home yesterday?   _____

  8. Were you downtown yesterday?   _____

CLOTHES

Frank will go shopping tomorrow. His wife's birthday
is next week, so he will buy a present for her.

COMPARE

He <u>will</u> go shopping <u>tomorrow</u>.

He <u>went</u> shopping <u>yesterday</u>.

PRACTICE

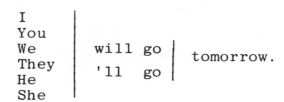

<u>Will</u> he go tomorrow?
    <u>Yes</u>, he <u>will</u>.
    <u>No</u>, he <u>won't</u>.

ANSWER THE QUESTIONS

1. Will he go shopping tomorrow?   Yes, *he will.*

2. Will he buy a present tomorrow?   No, _____

3. Will he go shopping next week?   Yes, _____

4. Will she buy a present for her daughter?   No, _____

5. Will they buy a present for their sons?   Yes, _____

6. Will you buy a present for your children?   _____

7. Will you buy a present for your friend?   _____

LISTEN TO THE STORY
FILL IN THE BLANKS

Frank _____ shopping yesterday.

He _____ to three stores.

He _____ at many things and

_____ the prices.

Next week is his wife's birthday.

He _____ a present

for _____.

TRUE OR FALSE?
WRITE "T" OR "F" in the blanks

1. *T* Frank went shopping yesterday.

2. ___ Frank went to two stores.

3. ___ Frank looked at many things.

4. ___ Frank bought something.

5. ___ Next week is his wife's birthday.

6. ___ He will buy a present for her.

He wanted to buy <u>some</u> jewelry.

He did <u>not</u> want to buy <u>any</u> jewelry.

<u>Did</u> he buy <u>any</u> jewelry?

FILL IN THE BLANKS

some   any

1. He wanted to buy *some* jewelry.

2. He wanted to buy _____ books.

3. Did he buy _____ pins?

4. He did not want to buy _____ games.

5. Did she buy _____ bracelets?

6. He did not want to buy _____ watches.

7. They did not want to buy _____ books.

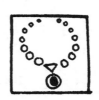

8. Did they buy _____ pins?

9. I wanted to buy _____ bracelets.

10. I did not want to buy _____ jewelry.

<u>Two Friends</u>

1. I need to buy some pots and pans.

2. You should go to _____.

1. Why?

2. Their pots and pans are on sale.

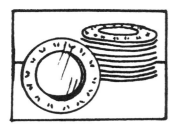

dishes

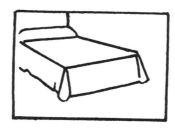

sheets

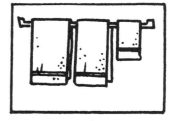

towels

WRITE SOME STORES IN YOUR CITY

_____   _____   _____

_____   _____   _____

WRITE CONVERSATIONS

1. I need to buy some _____.

2. You _____go to _____.

1. Why?

2. Their _____are on sale.

1. I need _____

2. You _____

1. Why?

2. _____

pots and pans

CLOTHES

You do not always have to pay cash in a store. You can charge, but you have to have a charge account or a credit card.

Charge accounts and credit cards are convenient. But you have to pay the total every month, or they are expensive.

CONVERSATION

Helen To The Clerk

1. Is this cash or charge?

2. Cash. I don't have a charge account.

1. Do you want one?

2. No, I don't. They are expensive. (Yes, I do. They are convenient.)

ANSWER THE QUESTIONS

1. Do you have to pay cash in a store?   *No, you don't.*

2. Can you charge?   _____

3. Do you need a credit card to charge?   _____

4. Do you have to pay every month?   _____

5. Does Helen have a charge account?   _____

6. Does she want one?   _____

7. Do you have a charge account?   _____

8. Do you want one?   _____

9. Why?   _____

LISTEN TO THE STORY ABOUT MARY
WRITE SENTENCES ABOUT THE STORY

1. department store

    The department store had a sale yesterday.

2. pots and pans

    _____

3. sheets and towels

    _____

4. bought

    _____

5. didn't buy

    _____

6. need

    _____

7. a lot of things

    _____

8. credit card

    _____

9. charge

    _____

10. cash

    _____

CLOTHES

TRANSPORTATION

Two Friends At The Bus Stop

1. Where are you going?

2. To work.
   I'm waiting for the bus.

1. Are you waiting for the local?

2. No. I'm taking the express.
   It's fast.

PRACTICE

I'm	
He's	waiting for the bus.
She's	

We're	
You're	waiting for the bus.
They're	

Is he going to work?
    Yes, he is.
    No, he isn't.

Is she going to work?
    Yes, she is.
    No, she isn't.

Are you taking the express?
    Yes, I am.
    No, I'm not.

Are they taking the express?
    Yes, they are.
    No, they aren't.

Are we taking the express?
    Yes, we are.
    No, we aren't.

ANSWER THE QUESTIONS

1. Where is he going?   *He is going to work.*

2. What is he waiting for?   _____

3. Is he waiting for the local?   _____

4. Is he taking the express?   _____

5. Is the express bus fast?   _____

6. Is the express bus slow?   _____

TRANSPORTATION

READ THE STORY

    John lives in the city.   He takes the bus to work.
He likes to take the express.   It's fast.

PRACTICE

He		takes the bus to work.	I		take the bus to work.
She			We		
			You		
			They		

He takes the bus	to work.
	to school.
	to the park.
	downtown.

WRITE ABOUT YOU

1.   I take the _____ to work.

2.   I take the _____ downtown.

3.   I take the _____ to school.

This is John's family.

PRACTICE

He	takes	his	car.
She		her	

I	take	my	car.
You		your	
We		our	
They		their	

FILL IN THE BLANKS

      my   his   her   our   your   their

1. He takes *his* _____ car.

2. She takes _____ car.

3. I take _____ car.

4. They take _____ car.

5. John takes _____ car.

6. John's mother and father take _____ car.

7. His aunt takes _____ car.

8. You and I take _____ car.

3

John lives in _____ .

He takes the _____ everywhere.

He takes the _____ to work.

He takes the _____ to the park.

He takes the _____ to his brother's house.

PRACTICE

Does John live here?

Yes, he does.

No, he doesn't.

WRITE QUESTIONS AND ANSWERS ABOUT JOHN

1. *Does John take the bus to work* ?
   Yes, he does.

2. _____ ?

   _____

3. _____ ?

   _____

WRITE ABOUT YOU

I live in _____ . I take the _____ to work.

I take the _____ to the park. I take the _____ to

_____ .

READ THE STORY
FILL IN THE BLANKS

Peggy lives in _____. She works downtown.
She takes the _____ to work every day. On
Sunday Peggy likes to go to the park. She goes
with her boyfriend. They take a _____.

PRACTICE

She goes with her <u>boyfriend</u>.   She goes with <u>him</u>.
         her sister   her
         her cousins   them
         you and me   us
         you   you
         me   me

CHANGE THE SENTENCES

her   him   us   them   me   you

1. She goes with her sister.

    She goes with her.

2. She goes with her cousins.

    _____

3. She goes with her brother.

    _____

4. She goes with her aunt.

    _____

5. She goes with you and me.

    _____

5

TRANSPORTATION

Two Friends

1. Do you live in the city?

2. Yes, I do.

1. Do you ride the bus?

2. No, I don't.
   I walk everywhere.

PRACTICE

<u>Do</u> you live in the city?

<u>Yes</u>, I <u>do</u>.

<u>No</u>, I <u>don't</u>.

ANSWER THE QUESTIONS

1. Do you live in the city? _____

2. Do you ride the bus to school? _____

3. Do you ride the bus to work? _____

4. Does John live in the city? _____

5. Does Peggy live in the city? _____

6. Does John take the bus to work? _____

7. Does Peggy take the bus to the park? _____

8. Do you ride the bus to the park? _____

READ THE STORY

Sam lives in the city. He always takes the bus to work. He usually takes the express. It's very fast. Sometimes the express is very crowded, so Sam takes the local. The local isn't very fast, but it's pretty fast.

PRACTICE

He | always / usually | takes the bus.

Sometimes | he takes the local.

FILL IN THE BLANKS

always   usually   sometimes

1. I *always* take the bus.

2. He _____ takes the express.

3. _____ she takes the local.

4. _____ the express is crowded.

5. The local bus is _____ slow.

6. The express bus is _____ fast.

WRITE ABOUT YOU

I live in _____ . I _____ take the _____ to work. I _____ take the _____ . It's very _____ .

CONVERSATION

To The Bus Driver

1. Do you go to the Greyhound station?

2. No, I don't.
   You have to transfer at _____Street.

1. Do you go to _____Street?

2. Sure. Get on.

PRACTICE

You have to | transfer
get off
wait
change buses | here.

I
We
You
They | have to get off here.

He
She | has to get off here.

WRITE places you want to go

Greyhound Station _____ _____

WRITE STREET NAMES

_____ _____ _____

WRITE A CONVERSATION

1. Do you go to _____?

2. No, I _____.
   You _____transfer at _____

1. Do you go to _____Street?

2. _____.

TRANSPORTATION

John has to go to _____ tomorrow. He is going to leave
here tomorrow morning. He is going to arrive in _____
tomorrow afternoon. He is going to take the bus.

PRACTICE

He is going to leave | tomorrow.
He is going to arrive | tomorrow morning.
| tomorrow afternoon.
| next week.

I am |
He is | going to go   tomorrow.
She is |

We |
You | are going to go   tomorrow.
They |

WRITE SENTENCES

1. I *am going to* _____ leave *next week* _____ .

2. They _____ arrive _____ .

3. She _____ go _____ .

4. We _____ leave _____ .

5. You _____ arrive _____ .

Two Friends

1. I'm going to go to New York next week.

2. Are you going to fly?

1. No, I'm not. It's too expensive.
    I'm going to take the bus.

PRACTICE

| Are you going to | take the bus? | Yes, I am. |
| | take the train? | |

| Are you going to | fly? | No, I'm not. |
| | drive? | |

It's too	slow.
	expensive.
	far.

WRITE CONVERSATIONS

1. I'm going to go to _____

2. Are you going to _____

1. No, _____. It's _____

    I'm going to _____

1. I'm _____

2. Are you _____

1. No, _____. It's _____

    I _____

Calling The Greyhound Station

1. Hello. Greyhound.
2. What time do buses leave for _____?
1. Morning, afternoon or night?
2. Afternoon.
1. 12:50, 3:15 and 6:00.
2. How long is the trip?
1. _____ hours.
2. How much is the fare?
1. $_____
2. Is that round trip or one way?
1. One way.
2. O. K. Thank you.

READ THE TIMETABLE

	leave	arrive	fare
Los Angeles	9:25 a.m.	8:36 p.m.	$25.00
Portland	7:15 a.m.	10:45 p.m.	$36.00
Seattle	6:05 p.m.	11:30 a.m.	$42.00
Vancouver	4:45 p.m.	2:10 p.m. next day	$60.00

ANSWER THE QUESTIONS

1. What time do buses leave for Los Angeles?   *9:25 a.m.*
2. How long is the trip?   _____
3. How much is the fare?   _____
4. What time do buses arrive in Seattle?   _____
5. How much is the fare to Vancouver?   _____

David went to _____ last week. He took a bus.

The trip was _____ hours long. The bus was very slow,

but it wasn't expensive.

PRACTICE

He <u>went</u> to _____.

He <u>took</u> a bus.

The bus <u>was</u> slow.

slow   fast

expensive   cheap

I went to _____.

I took a _____.

The _____ was _____.

I_____

I_____

The_____

clean   dirty

crowded   empty

12

Two Friends

1. I went to New York.

2. Did you fly?

1. No, I didn't. I took the bus.
   It was slow, but it wasn't
   expensive.

PRACTICE

Did you fly?

Yes, I did.

No, I didn't.

ANSWER THE QUESTIONS

1. Did you fly?   Yes, *I did.*

2. Did you walk?   No, _____

3. Did you take the car?   No, _____

4. Did you drive?   Yes, _____

5. Did you take the bus?   No, _____

6. Did you take the train?   Yes, _____

WRITE A CONVERSATION

1. I went to _____

2. Did you _____

1. No, I _____. I _____

   It _____, but it _____

John wanted to go downtown yesterday. He didn't want to walk. He waited for the bus, but it didn't come. So he walked downtown.

PRACTICE

He <u>wanted</u> to go downtown | last week.
yesterday.

He <u>waited</u> for | the bus.
the express.

He <u>didn't want</u> to | walk.
take a taxi.

<u>Did</u> he go downtown?

    <u>Yes</u>, he <u>did</u>.   <u>No</u>, he <u>didn't</u>.

ANSWER THE QUESTIONS

1. Did John want to go downtown yesterday?   *Yes, he did*
2. Did he want to walk?
3. Did he want to take the bus?
4. Did he want to take a taxi?
5. Did he wait for the bus?
6. Did the bus come?

TRANSPORTATION

Two Friends At Work

1. I want to go to _____, but I can't drive.

2. You can take the bus.
    It's not expensive.

1. The local bus?

2. No, silly. The Greyhound.

PRACTICE

You can take | the plane.
the bus.
the train.

I
He
She
We
You
They | can take the bus.

I can't | walk.
drive.
run.
fly.

FINISH THE SENTENCES

1. I want to go to *New York*, but *I can't walk.*

2. I want to go to _____, but _____

3. He wants _____, but _____

4. They want_____, but _____

5. She _____, but _____

Two Friends

1. Can I catch the express here?

2. No, you can't.
   You have to go to the next corner.

1. Why?

2. It stops only at some corners.

PRACTICE

Can I catch the bus here?

Yes, you can.

No, you can't.

ANSWER THE QUESTIONS
USE THESE WORDS

can	do	did
can't	don't	didn't

1. Can you drive?   Yes, _I can._

2. Did you walk?   Yes, _____

3. Do you take the bus?   No, _____

4. Did you fly?   No, _____

5. Can you take the express?   No, _____

6. Do you ride the local?   Yes, _____

Two Friends

1. Can I go now?

2. Yes, you can.

   The sign says "Walk".

    1. Can I go there?

    2. No, you can't.

       The sign says "Do Not Enter".

READ THE SIGNS

WRITE CONVERSATIONS

1. _____I_____?

2. Yes, _____

   The sign says _____

    1. _____I_____?

    2. No, _____

       The sign says _____

ANSWER THE QUESTIONS

1.   Which bus goes to the train station?   _#30_____

2.   Which bus goes to the Greyhound station?   _____

3.   Which bus goes to the civic center?   _____

WRITE QUESTIONS AND ANSWERS
USE "which"

1.   _Which bus goes to the civic center?_
        _The # 47._____

2.   _____
     _____

3.   _____
     _____

4.   _____
     _____

TRANSPORTATION

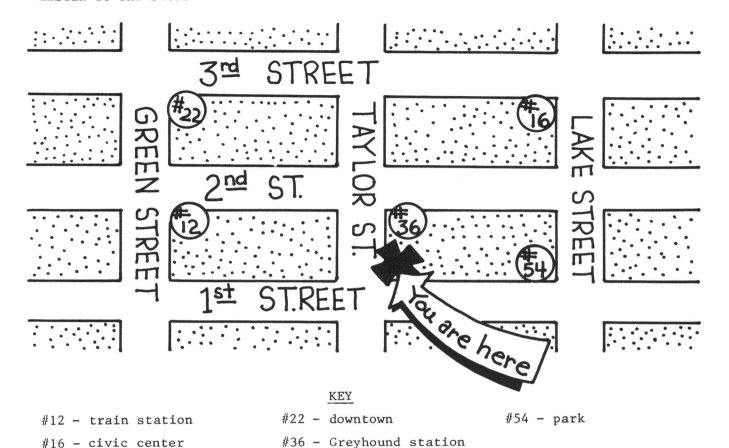

KEY

#12 - train station   #22 - downtown   #54 - park

#16 - civic center   #36 - Greyhound station

CONVERSATION   <u>On The Street</u>

1. Excuse me. Which bus goes to the train station?
2. The #12.
1. Where is the bus stop?
2. Walk one block.
   Turn left.
   It's at Second and Green Street.
1. Thank you.

PRACTICE

Turn	left.		Walk	one block.
	right.			two blocks.

It's at	Second	and	Green	Street.
	Third		Taylor	
	First		Lake	

19   *TRANSPORTATION*

POST OFFICE

PRACTICE

| He | | a stamp. |
| She | is buying | a money order. |

<u>Is</u> he buying a stamp?
  <u>Yes</u>, he <u>is</u>.
  <u>No</u>, he isn't.

ANSWER THE QUESTIONS

1. Is Tom in the post office?   *Yes, he is.*

2. Is he buying a stamp?

3. Is he buying a money order?

4. Is the money order for his brother?

5. Is it for his sister?

READ THE STORY

Tom's sister is a student in Japan. He sends money to her every month. He goes to the post office and buys a money order.

PRACTICE

He sends money to <u>his sister</u>.
    He sends money to <u>her</u>.

He sends money to <u>his brother</u>.
    He sends money to <u>him</u>.

He sends money to <u>his parents</u>.
    He sends money to <u>them</u>.

He sends money to <u>you</u>.

He sends money to <u>me</u>.

He sends money to <u>you and me</u>.
    He sends money to <u>us</u>.

WRITE SENTENCES

her   him   them
you   me   us

1. Tom sends money to his sister.

    He sends money to her.

2. Tom sends money to his parents.

    _____

3. Tom sends money to his brother.

    _____

4. Tom sends money to you and me.

    _____

5. Tom sends money to you.

    _____

NOW

He <u>is buying</u> a money order now.

She <u>is going</u> to the post office now.

I <u>am sending</u> money now.

They <u>are getting</u> postcards now.

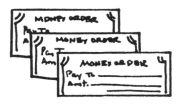

He <u>buys</u> a money order every day.

She <u>goes</u> to the post office every week.

I <u>send</u> money every month.

They <u>get</u> postcards every year.

WRITE SENTENCES

1. I   post office   now

I am going to the post office now.

2. He   send   every week

_____

3. She   money order   now

_____

4. They   postcards   every month

_____

5. You   envelopes   now

_____

To A Friend

1. Do you send money to your sister?

2. Yes, I do. Every month.

1. Do you send cash?

2. No, I don't.
   I never send cash by mail.

PRACTICE

Do you send money to your sister?

Yes, I do.

No, I don't.

I never send cash by mail.

I always buy a money order.

ANSWER THE QUESTIONS

1. Do you send money to your family?   _____

2. Do you send money every month?   _____

3. Do you send cash by mail?   _____

4. Do you send money to your sister?   _____

5. Do you send money to your parents?   _____

6. Do you send money to your cousin?   _____

7. Do you send money every day?   _____

FILL IN THE BLANKS

always   never

1. I _____ send cash by mail.

2. I _____ send money to my parents.

3. I _____ send a money order by mail.

4

Bob has a good job and he likes to help his family.
He sends money to them every month. But he doesn't send cash.
He always sends a cashier's check or a money order.

PRACTICE

Does Bob have a good job?
   Yes, he does.
   No, he doesn't.

ANSWER THE QUESTIONS

1. Does Bob have a good job?   *Yes, he does.*
2. Does Bob send cash to his family?   _____
3. Does he help his family?   _____
4. Does Bob send cash to his sister?   _____
5. Does Bob send a money order?   _____
6. Do you send cash by mail?   _____
7. Do you send money orders?   _____
8. Do you help your family?   _____

5

<u>To A Friend</u>

1.   I'm going to the post office.
     Do you need any stamps?

2.   No, but I need some postcards.

1.   How many?

2.   A couple.

1.   O. K.

PRACTICE

I need <u>some</u> | stamps.
               | postcards.
               | airletters.

I <u>don't</u> need <u>any</u> | stamps.
                      | envelopes.
                      | postcards.

<u>Do</u> you need <u>any</u> | stamps?
                    | airletters?

<u>How many</u> stamps do you need?
          Five.
          Ten.
          A couple.
          A dozen.

FILL IN THE BLANKS

                    some   any

1.   I need *some* stamps.   5.   I need _____ money orders.

2.   I don't need _____ envelopes.   6.   I need _____

3.   I need _____ airletters.   7.   I don't need _____

4.   I don't need _____ stamps.   8.   _____

CONVERSATION   <u>To A Friend</u>

1. What's this?

2. It's a notice from the post office.
    You have a package.

1. Where is it?

2. It's at the post office.
    You have to get it.

COMPARE AND PRACTICE

I You We They	<u>have</u>	a package. a letter. a notice.

He She	<u>has</u>	a package. a letter.

I You We They	<u>have to</u>	go to the post office. get a package.

He She	<u>has to</u>	go. get it.

FILL IN THE BLANKS

       has   have

       has to   have to

1. I _*have to*_ go to the post office.

2. He _____ a notice.

3. You _____ a package.

4. They _____ get a package.

5. He _____ get it.

6. We _____ a letter.

7. She _____ get a package.

Marge got a package from Japan. It came yesterday. She went to the post office and got it. But she had to pay duty. She was happy to get the package, but she wasn't happy to pay duty.

PRACTICE

The package
The letter
The telegram
The notice

<u>came</u> yesterday.

Marge <u>went</u> to the post office

last week.
yesterday.
Monday.

She <u>had to</u> pay duty yesterday.

She <u>was</u> happy to get the package.

She <u>wasn't</u> happy to pay duty.

WRITE A CONVERSATION

1. I _____ to the post office yesterday.

2. Why?

1. I _____ a _____ from _____

2. That's nice.

1. I _____ pay $_____ duty.

2. That's too bad.

<u>To A Friend</u>

1.   Did you get a package yesterday?

2.   Yes, I did.

1.   Did you have to pay duty?

2.   No, I didn't.

PRACTICE

Did you get | a package | yesterday?
            | a letter |
            | a telegram |
            | a phone call |

<u>Yes</u>, I <u>did</u>.

<u>No</u>, I <u>didn't</u>.

WRITE QUESTIONS AND ANSWERS

did   didn't

1. <u>Did</u> you get a package yesterday?   *No, I didn't.*

2. _____ you have to pay duty?   _____

3. _____ get a letter last week?   _____

4. _____ you get a _____ last month?   _____

5. _____ yesterday?   _____

6. _____ pay duty?   _____

7. _____?   _____

8. _____?   _____

9. _____?   _____

10. _____?   _____

Dan moved last week, but his mail didn't. It stayed at his old address. He wanted it at his new address, so he went to the post office. He filled out a change of address card. Now his mail comes to his new address.

PRACTICE

Dan <u>moved</u> | last month.
| last week.
| Saturday.

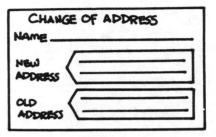

His mail <u>didn't come</u> | yesterday.
| last week.

He		his mail.		We			our mail.
She	<u>wanted</u>	her mail.		You	<u>wanted</u>	your mail.
I		my mail.		They			their mail.

READ THE STORY

Lucy moved last week, too. She went to the post office. She filled out a card. Her mail came.

WRITE ABOUT DAN AND LUCY

1. Dan moved last week.

   Lucy _____ last week, too.

2. Dan didn't go to the post office.

   Lucy _____ to the post office.

3. Dan didn't fill out a card.

   Lucy _____ a card.

4. Dan's mail didn't come.

   Lucy's mail _____.

Ann is going to move next week. Tomorrow she is going to go to the post office. She is going to fill out a change of address card.

PRACTICE

She He	is going to move	next week. tomorrow.

I	am going to move	tomorrow.

We You They	are going to move	next year. next month.

<u>Is</u> he going to move tomorrow?   <u>Are</u> you going to move?

     <u>Yes</u>, he <u>is</u>.   <u>Yes</u>, I <u>am</u>.
     <u>No</u>, he <u>isn't</u>.   <u>No</u>, I'<u>m not</u>.

<u>Are</u> they going to move?
<u>Yes</u>, they <u>are</u>.
<u>No</u>, they <u>aren't</u>.

WRITE SENTENCES

tomorrow   next week   next month   next year

1. I *I am going to move next month.*

2. He _____

3. They _____

4. You _____

5. She _____

To The Clerk

1. This letter is going
    airmail to _____

    I want to register it.

2. Here is your receipt.
    Keep it.

1. O. K. How much?

2. $_____.

    $_____to register
    the letter and $_____
    for stamps.

1. This package is going regular
    mail to _____.

    I want to insure it for $50.

2. Here is your receipt.
    Keep it.

1. O. K. How much?

2. $_____.

    $_____ to insure it and
    $_____for postage.

PRACTICE

This package is going | airmail <br> regular mail | to _____.

I want to insure this package <u>for</u> | $50.
 $100.

| I
 You
 We
 They | <u>want to</u> | register it. | He
 She | <u>wants to</u> insure it. |

<u>How much</u> is it?

    $_____to insure it. $_____for stamps.

    $_____to register it. $_____for postage.

WRITE A CONVERSATION

1. This _____is going _____mail to _____.

    How much is it?

2. _____. _____

<u>To The Clerk</u>

1. This package is going to Europe. Should I insure it?

2. Is it valuable?

1. Yes, it is.

2. Then you should insure it.

1. This letter is going to Hong Kong. Should I register it?

2. Is it valuable?

1. No, it isn't.

2. Then you shouldn't register it. It's expensive.

PRACTICE

You <u>should</u> | register it.
            | insure it.

You <u>shouldn't</u> | register it.
               | insure it.

<u>Should</u> I register it?

    <u>Yes</u>, you <u>should</u>.
    <u>No</u>, you <u>shouldn't</u>.

WRITE A CONVERSATION

1. This _____ is going to _____.
   _____ I insure it?

2. _____ valuable?

1. _____

2. Then _____

To A Friend

1.   Should I seal this package?

2.   Are you going to insure it?

1.   Yes, I am.   It's valuable.

2.   Then you should seal it.

1.   Should I seal this package?

2.   Are you going to insure it?

1.   No, I'm not.   It isn't valuable.

2.   Then you shouldn't seal it.
     It costs less.

| Should | she he I we you they | seal this package? |

1.   _____this package?

2.   _____insure it?

1.   _____

2.   Then _____

     _____

<u>To The Clerk</u>

1. I'm mailing an important letter overseas.
    Can I insure it?

2. No, you can't.

1. Can I register it?

2. Yes, you can.

1. How much does it cost?

2. $_____.

1. O. K. Thank you.

PRACTICE

I		
He		
She	<u>can</u>	register it.
We		
You		
They		

I		
He		
She	<u>can't</u>	insure it.
We		
You		
They		

<u>Can</u> I register it?

    <u>Yes</u>, you <u>can</u>.
    <u>No</u>, you <u>can't</u>.

WRITE A CONVERSATION

1. I'm mailing _____

    _____?

2. No, _____

1. _____?

2. Yes, _____

<u>To A Friend</u>

1. You can't mail this letter.

2. Why not?

1. The address is wrong.

2. What's wrong with it?

1. Everything. This is how
   you write an address in English.

What's wrong?

The	address	is wrong.
	name	
	zip code	
	return address	

16   POST OFFICE

To A Friend

1. I'm going to the post office.

2. I need some airletters.

1. I'll get you some.

2. Good. I need 20.

1. Wow! That's a lot of airletters.

2. Well, I write a lot of letters
   and airletters are cheap.

PRACTICE

I need <u>some</u> | envelopes.
airletters.
stamps.

I'll get you <u>some</u>.

That's <u>a lot of</u> | postcards.
airletters.
stamps.

WRITE CONVERSATIONS

1. I'm going to the post office.

2. I need _____

1. I'll _____

2. Good. I need _____

1. _____!

2. Well, _____

1. I'm going _____

2. I need _____

1. I'll _____

To A Friend

1. I'll get you some stamps.
   How many do you need?

2. Five.

1. That's not many.

2. Well, I don't write many letters.

PRACTICE

How many | envelopes
         | stamps | do you need?
         | airletters

I don't write many | cards.
                   | letters.
                   | airletters.

That's not many.

FILL IN THE BLANKS

            a lot of   many

1. I write _____ letters

2. I don't write _____ postcards.

3. I need _____ stamps.

4. I don't need _____ envelopes.

5. I need _____ airletters.

6. I don't want _____ stamps.

7. I _____ letters.

8. I _____ postcards.

<u>To A Friend</u>

1.   How many stamps did you buy?

2.   Five.

1.   How much money did you spend?

2. $_____.

1.   Did you send the package?

2.   Yes, I did.

1.   How much did it weigh?

2.   Two pounds.

1.   How much did it cost?

2. $_____.

PRACTICE

How many	airletters postcards stamps	did you buy?

How much	did it weigh? money did you spend? did it cost?

WRITE QUESTIONS

            How much   How many

1.   20
    How many stamps did you buy?

2.   2 pounds

_____

3. $1.00

_____

4.   6

_____

To A Friend

1. I'm mad.

2. Why?

1. I waited for an hour
   in the post office.

2. What for?

1. I needed a few stamps.

2. Buy a lot of stamps.
   You'll save time.

PRACTICE

I needed <u>a few</u> | envelopes.
                       | stamps.
                       | airletters.

Buy <u>a lot of</u> | postcards.
                      | stamps.
                      | airletters.

I'm | mad.
      | annoyed.
      | angry.
      | upset.

FILL IN THE BLANKS

        a lot of   a few   many   some

1. I write _____letters.

2. I don't write _____postcards.

3. Buy _____stamps. You'll save time.

4. I don't write many letters. I need _____airletters.

5. I write a lot of cards. I need _____postcards.

6. I don't write many letters. I need _____stamps.

We _____ to the post office for _____ things.
(1)   (2)

We _____ stamps, _____ and _____ at
(3)   (4)   (5)

the post office. We _____ to the post office to _____
(6)   (7)

packages and to _____ packages. We _____ money
(8)   (9)

orders _____ post office, too.
(10)

WRITE A STORY ABOUT YOU

I _____ the post office for _____ things.
(1)   (2)

I buy _____, _____ and _____
(3)   (4)   (5)

at the post office.

I mail _____ at the post office.
(6)

I get _____ at the post office.
(7)

Sometimes I buy _____ at the post office, too.
(8)

FILL IN THE BLANKS

This ___*is*___ the Chan family. They _____ all going to
    (1)   *(2)*

school this year. Mr. and Mrs. Chan _____ to adult school.
                                        (3)

Tommy _____ going to college and Janet _____ to high school.
      (4)   *(5)*

Mr. and Mrs. Chan _____ to adult school. They _____
                         (6)   *(7)*

English. Mr. Chan _____ to his class at night. Mrs. Chan
                      (8)

_____ in the morning.
   (9)

1

<u>A Friend To Mr. Chan</u>

      1.   Do you study English?

      2.   Yes, I do.

      1.   Where?

      2.   At adult school.

PRACTICE

    <u>Do</u> you study English?
      <u>Yes</u>, I <u>do</u>.

    <u>Where</u> do you study English?
      At _____School.
      Here.

ANSWER THE QUESTIONS

1. Do you study English?   _____

2. Do you like it?   _____

3. Where do you study **English**?   _____

4. Do you like your school?   _____

5. Is English easy?   _____

WRITE QUESTIONS

    1.   _____you study English?

    2.   _____do you _____English?

    3.   _____this school?

    4.   _____English easy?

                                              SCHOOL

Mr. Chan To A Friend

1. Do you go to English class in the morning?

2. No, I don't.

1. When do you go?

2. At night.

PRACTICE

Do you go to class | in the morning?
in the afternoon?   No, I don't.
in the evening?

When do you go to class?

In the morning.   At night.
In the afternoon.   At 8:00.
In the evening.   At 6:30.

WRITE CONVERSATIONS

1. Do you study English?

2. _____

1. Where do you study?

2. _____

1. When do you go to class?

2. _____

1. _____you study _____?

2. _____

1. _____do you study?

2. _____

1. _____do you go to class?

2. _____

Mr. Chan studies English at adult school. His son, Tommy, studies English, too. But he studies in college.

Tommy takes English, accounting and history. Mr. Chan just takes English. That's enough!

CONVERSATION   <u>To A Friend</u>

    1. Do you go to college?

    2. No, I don't.
        I go to adult school.

    1. What do you take?

    2. English.

PRACTICE

<u>Do</u> you go to | high school?
| college?   No, I <u>don't</u>.
| adult school?

What do you take?

I take | English.
| typing.
| history.
| citizenship.
| business.

ANSWER THE QUESTIONS

1. Do you go to adult school? _____

2. Do you go to a university? _____

3. Do you take typing? _____

4. Do you take English? _____

5. Do you take citizenship? _____

6. What do you take? _____

4

<u>To A Friend</u>

1.   Does your wife take citizenship now?

2.   Yes, she does.

1.   Does she take English, too?

2.   No, she doesn't.
     She already speaks English pretty well.

<u>Does</u> she like her class?

   <u>Yes</u>, she <u>does</u>.   It's | interesting.
                                        | fun.
                                        | easy.

   <u>No</u>, she <u>doesn't</u>. It's | boring.
                                        | hard.
                                        | difficult.

She <u>already</u> speaks English <u>pretty well</u>.

1. Does she like her class?   1. Does he like his class?

2. _____   2. _____

1. Why?   1. Why?

2. _____   2. _____

1. Do they like their class?   1. Do you like your class?

2. _____   2. _____

1. Why?   1. Why?

2. _____   2. _____

<u>To A Friend</u>

      1. Do you speak English?

      2. Yes, I do. A little.

      1. Does your wife speak English?

      2. Yes, she does.

PRACTICE

I		Chinese.
We	speak <u>a little</u>	English.
You		Spanish.
They		

He	speaks <u>a lot of</u>	Vietnamese.
She		Japanese.

ANSWER THE QUESTIONS

1. Do you speak English?   _____

2. Does your wife speak English?   _____

3. Does your husband speak English? _____

4. Do your children speak English?   _____

5. Do you speak Chinese?   _____

6. Do you speak Spanish?   _____

ASK YOUR CLASSMATE QUESTIONS
WRITE HIS OR HER ANSWERS

1. Does your classmate speak English? _____

2. Does he (she) speak Chinese?   _____

3. Does he (she) speak Spanish?   _____

4. What does he (she) speak?   _____

READ THE STORY

Mr. Chan's English class went on a trip yesterday. They
went downtown and visited some stores. They talked to new people.
They practiced new words. Mr. Chan had a lot of fun and he learned
a lot, too.

COMPARE AND PRACTICE

every day

They <u>go</u> downtown every day.
They <u>visit</u> stores every day.
They <u>talk</u> to people every day.
They <u>see</u> new people every day.
They <u>meet</u> new people every day.
They <u>practice</u> new words every day.
They <u>learn</u> new words every day.

yesterday

They <u>went</u> downtown yesterday.
They visit<u>ed</u> stores yesterday.
They talk<u>ed</u> to people yesterday.
They <u>saw</u> new people yesterday.
They <u>met</u> new people yesterday.
They practic<u>ed</u> words yesterday.
They learn<u>ed</u> new words yesterday.

WRITE A STORY

Mr. _____'s class _____ downtown yesterday.
　　　　　　(1)　　　　　　　　　　(2)

They _____ some new people. They _____ stores.
　　　　　　(3)　　　　　　　　　　　　　　　　　　　(4)

They _____ some new words. Mr. _____ had a lot of fun, and
　　　　　(5)　　　　　　　　　　　　　　　　(6)

he _____ a lot, too.
　　　(7)

7   *SCHOOL*

<u>To A Friend</u>

   1.   I had fun in school today.

   2.   What did you do?

   1.   I went on a trip.

   2.   Did you learn anything?

   1.   Yes, I did.   I learned a lot of new words.
        I practiced English with some new people.

PRACTICE

What <u>did</u> you <u>do</u>?

   I <u>went</u> on a trip.

   I <u>had</u> fun.

   I <u>learned</u> new words.

<u>Did</u> you <u>learn</u> anything?

   <u>Yes</u>, I <u>did</u>.

   <u>No</u>, I <u>didn't</u>.

ANSWER THE QUESTIONS

1.   Did Mr. Chan go on a trip yesterday?   *Yes, he did* _____

2.   Did he go downtown?   _____

3.   Did he have fun?   _____

4.   Did he learn new words?   _____

5.   Did he talk to some new people?   _____

6.   Did you go on a trip last week?   _____

7.   Did you go downtown last weekend?   _____

8.   Did you practice English yesterday?   _____

9.   Did you learn new words yesterday?   _____

Schools are different in every country. In some countries, students have to pay tuition. They have to wear a uniform. But in the United States they don't. They don't have to pay tuition. They don't have to wear a uniform.

PRACTICE

I		
We	have to pay tuition.	
You		
They		

He
She   has to pay tuition.

I		
We	don't have to pay tuition.	
You		
They		

He
She   doesn't have to pay tuition.

WRITE ABOUT THE UNITED STATES

Students in the United States _____ wear a uniform.

They _____ pay tuition.

WRITE ABOUT YOUR COUNTRY

I come from _____.

Students in _____ wear a uniform.

They _____ pay tuition.

Janet To Her Mother

1. Hey, Mom.
    I have to buy a gym suit.

2. Why?

1. I need it for P. E.

2. But you already have
    tennis shoes.

1. I know.
    But I need a gym suit, too.

PRACTICE

I have to buy | <u>a</u> | pen.
gym suit.
notebook.

I have to buy | <u>some</u> | paper.
tennis shoes.
pencils.

FINISH THE SENTENCES

some   a

1. I have to buy _____tennis shoes.

2. I have to buy _____gym suit.

3. She has to buy _____pen.

4. He has to buy _____pens.

5. They have to buy _____paper.

6. You have to buy _____notebook.

7. I have to buy _____

8. He _____

9. You _____

Public schools are free in the United States. Students don't have to pay tuition. They don't have to wear uniforms.

Students in the United States don't have a lot of homework. They are usually noisy in class. They don't sit quietly. Sometimes they talk and laugh in the classroom.

PRACTICE

	always	
They are	usually	noisy.
	sometimes	
	never	

Sometimes	they are quiet.

FILL IN THE BLANKS

always   usually   sometimes   never

I come from _____

1. Students are _____noisy in the United States.

    Students are _____noisy in _____.

2. Students are _____quiet in the United States.

    Students are _____quiet in _____.

3. _____they laugh in the classroom in the United States.

    They _____laugh in the classroom in _____.

4. Students in my class are _____noisy.

5. Students in my class are _____quiet.

6. Students in my son's class are _____quiet.

7. Students in my daughter's class are _____noisy.

8. At home my children are _____quiet.

CONVERSATION   Parent To A Friend

1. Does your son like school?

2. He likes it, but I don't.

1. Why not?

2. The students are always noisy
    and they don't have any homework.

PRACTICE

He She	likes it, but I don't.	You They	like it, but I don't.

I We You They	don't have <u>any</u> homework.	He She	doesn't have <u>any</u> homework.

ANSWER THE QUESTIONS

1. Does your son like school?

    He _____ it, but I _____.

2. Does your daughter like school?

    She _____ it, but I _____.

3. Do your children like school?

    They _____, but _____.

4. Do the students like school?

    _____, but _____.

5. Does your friend like school?

    _____, but _____.

12

Child To Parent

1. Can I go play?

2. Do you have any homework?

1. No, I don't have any.

2. O. K. You can go play.

1. Can I go play?

2. Do you have any homework?

1. Yes, I have some.

2. No, you can't go play.
    Do your homework!

PRACTICE

Do you have <u>any</u> homework?

Yes, I have <u>some</u>.

No, I <u>don't</u> have <u>any</u>.

<u>Can</u> I go play?

<u>Yes</u>, you <u>can</u>.
<u>No</u>, you <u>can't</u>.

WRITE CONVERSATIONS

1. _____ I go play?

2. Do you have _____ homework?

1. Yes, _____

2. No, you _____

    Do _____ !

1. _____ I _____ ?

2. Do you have _____ homework?

1. _____

2. O. K. _____

Two Students

   1.   I'm going to watch TV tonight.
        Are you?

   2.   No, I'm not.
        I'm going to study.

   1.   Why?

   2.   I'm going to have a test tomorrow.

PRACTICE

I'm He's She's We're You're They're	going to watch TV	tomorrow. tonight this weekend.

Are you going to watch TV tonight?

No, I'm going to	study play cards relax listen to music go to school	tonight.

WRITE QUESTIONS AND ANSWERS

1. *Are* you *going to* play cards tonight?

   No, *I'm going to watch TV.*

2. _____ he _____ study this weekend?

   No, _____

3. _____ they _____ tomorrow?

   No, _____

4. _____

   _____

5. _____

   _____

Some students don't like to study, but Mrs. Chan does. She is a very good student. The teacher is proud of her. But sometimes the teacher asks her a question. She forgets the answer. Then she is embarrassed.

PRACTICE

I'm
He's
She's
We're
You're
They're

embarrassed.

She is a good student.   The teacher is proud of her.
He is a good student.   The teacher is proud of him.
You are a good student.   The teacher is proud of you.
I am a good student.   The teacher is proud of me.
We are good students.   The teacher is proud of us.
They are good students.   The teacher is proud of them.

WRITE CONVERSATIONS

1. I'm embarrassed.

2. Why?

1. The teacher says _____a good student.

2. Don't be embarrassed. Be proud of _____.

        1. I'm embarrassed.

        2. Why?

        1. The teacher says _____a good student.

        2. Don't be embarrassed. Be proud of _____.

<u>To A Friend</u>

1. I'm worried about my son.

2. What's wrong with him?

1. He's lazy and doesn't do his homework.

2. Maybe he needs help. You should talk to his counselor.

1. I'm worried about my daughter.

2. What's wrong with her?

1. She's intelligent and she studies a lot. But her grades aren't good.

2. Maybe she needs help in English. You should get a tutor.

PRACTICE

I'm worried about my │ daughter.
                     │ son.
                     │ children.

He's │ lazy.
      │ hard-working.
      │ smart.
      │ intelligent.

You <u>should</u> talk to │ her teacher.
                     │ his counselor.
                     │ their tutor.

WRITE A CONVERSATION

1. I'm worried about my _____ .

2. What's wrong with _____ ?

1. _____

_____ _____

2. Maybe _____

You should _____

PTA BAKE SALE

What?   A Bake Sale

When?   This Friday 12-3 p.m.

Where?   Jackson School

Please come and bring your cakes, cupcakes and cookies. Help us earn money to buy books for the library.

ANSWER THE QUESTIONS

1. When is the bake sale?   _____

2. Where is the bake sale?   _____

3. Are they going to earn money?   _____

4. Are they going to buy books?   _____

5. Does the PTA help the school?   _____

6. Are you going to the bake sale?   _____

7. What are you going to bring?   _____

1. What's your favorite sport?	1. What's your favorite sport?
2. Football.	2. Basketball.
1. Can you play?	1. Can you play?
2. Of course.	2. No, I just watch.

PRACTICE

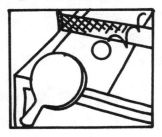

1   Football

2   Basketball

3   Tennis

4   Ping-pong

5   Baseball

6   Volleyball

<u>Can</u> you play basketball?

<u>Yes</u>, I <u>can</u>.	<u>No</u>, I <u>can't</u>.
Sure.	I just watch.
Of course.	Not at all.
A little.	

ANSWER THE QUESTIONS

1. What's your favorite sport?   _____

2. Can you play?   _____

3. What's your classmate's
    favorite sport?   _____

4. Can he (she) play?   _____

Two Students

    1. Can you play tennis?

    2. Yes, I can.

    1. Let's play this afternoon.

    2. I can't play this afternoon.
       I have to study.

PRACTICE

Can you play	now?
	tomorrow?
	this afternoon?
	this weekend?
	Saturday?

FINISH THE CONVERSATIONS

1. Let's play *baseball* this afternoon.

2. I can't play this afternoon. I have to *work.*

1. Let's play _____this weekend.

2. I can't play this weekend. I have to _____

1. Let's play _____

2. I can't play _____. I have to _____

1. Let's _____

2. I _____. I have to_____

1. Let's _____

2. I _____. I _____

CONVERSATION   Child To Parent

1. Mom, I need a note for my teacher.

2. Why?

1. Because I was absent yesterday.

PRACTICE

I was │ absent │ yesterday.
      │ out   │
      │ sick   │

This is Mrs. Chan's note:

> Dear Mrs. Baker,
>   Janet was absent yesterday.
> She couldn't go to school
> because she had a cold.
>   Yours truly,
>   May Chan

PRACTICE

She couldn't go to school because │ she was sick.
                                            │ she had a cold.
                                            │ she had a sore throat.

WRITE A NOTE TO YOUR TEACHER

The Chans came to the United States last year. They came from Hong Kong. School is very different in the United States.

The Chans don't have to pay tuition. Everyone can go to school. The teachers are friendly and they don't give a lot of homework.

High school and elementary school students aren't serious. They talk in the classroom. They don't have to wear uniforms.

But the Chans like American schools. They can study many things. They can study at night or in the morning and they go to a school near their house.

WRITE A STORY ABOUT YOU

I came to the United States _____. I came from

_____. School _____ very different in the United

States.

I _____ pay tuition. The teachers _____ friendly.

They _____ a lot of homework.

I _____ American schools. I can study _____.

I can study _____. I go to a school _____ my house.